A TRUE BOOK™

DISCARD

The Most Endangered
Elephants

KATIE MARSICO

Children's Press®
An Imprint of Scholastic Inc.

Content Consultant
Dr. Stephen S. Ditchkoff
Professor of Wildlife Sciences
Auburn University, Auburn, Alabama

Library of Congress Cataloging-in-Publication Data
Names: Marsico, Katie, 1980– author.
Title: Elephants / by Katie Marsico.
Other titles: True book.
Description: New York, NY : Children's Press, 2017. | Series: A true book | Includes bibliographical
   references and index.
Identifiers: LCCN 2016026621| ISBN 9780531227275 (library binding) | ISBN 9780531232781 (pbk.)
Subjects: LCSH: Elephants—Juvenile literature. | Endangered species—Juvenile literature. |
   Wildlife conservation—Juvenile literature.
Classification: LCC QL737.P98 M3698 2017 | DDC 599.67—dc23
LC record available at https://lccn.loc.gov/2016026621

© 2017 Scholastic Inc.
All rights reserved. Published in 2017 by Children's Press, an imprint of Scholastic Inc.
Printed in China 62

SCHOLASTIC, CHILDREN'S PRESS, A TRUE BOOK™, and associated logos are trademarks and/or
registered trademarks of Scholastic Inc.
1 2 3 4 5 6 7 8 9 10 R 26 25 24 23 22 21 20 19 18 17

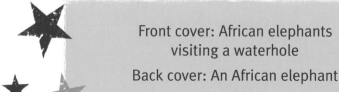

Front cover: African elephants
visiting a waterhole
Back cover: An African elephant

Find the Truth!

Everything you are about to read is true *except* for one of the sentences on this page.

Which one is **TRUE**?

T or F Elephants may live up to 70 years in the wild.

T or F Poaching never occurs in protected areas.

Find the answers in this book.

Contents

THE **BIG** TRUTH!

Big Animal, Big Impact

Elephant with
a tracking collar

Elephants greeting each other

Asian elephant

5

Two rangers ride an elephant as they patrol Kaziranga National Park in India.

CHAPTER 1

Rangers to the Rescue

Elephants are Earth's largest land animals. Size, however, doesn't shield these mammals from **poachers**. Fortunately, wildlife rangers are fighting to protect elephants.

One of a ranger's roles is to monitor elephant populations in protected areas such as national parks. These spaces are set aside to support **conservation** efforts. Their boundaries, however, aren't always enough to keep poachers away.

More than 50 percent of wild Asian elephants live in India.

A Dangerous Job

Poachers often kill elephants for ivory. Ivory is a hard, white substance that forms the main part of an elephant's **tusks**. It is used to make everything from statues to jewelry to eating utensils. Currently, the sale and purchase of ivory products is banned internationally. Nevertheless, illegal hunting and trade continue to threaten elephants. Rangers have the difficult and dangerous responsibility of guarding these animals against poachers.

Items made from ivory are usually expensive. In turn, the profit drives poachers and other people involved in illegal trade.

As rangers keep watch over elephants, they themselves face many risks. They work in remote locations, or places that are far from cities and towns. There, both weather and wildlife sometimes prove unpredictable. Rangers are also frequently involved in life-and-death conflicts with poachers. People eager to kill elephants for ivory don't want anyone to stand in their way. In some cases, hunters have even murdered rangers.

Park rangers patrol the Virunga National Park in the Democratic Republic of Congo.

An Overview of Elephants

There are two species of elephant. African elephants are one of them. They roam 37 countries throughout the Congo Basin and coastal East Africa. Experts divide African elephants into two subspecies: savanna and forest. Savanna elephants spend most of their time in grassy plains and woodlands. Forest elephants, on the other hand, live in Africa's rain forests.

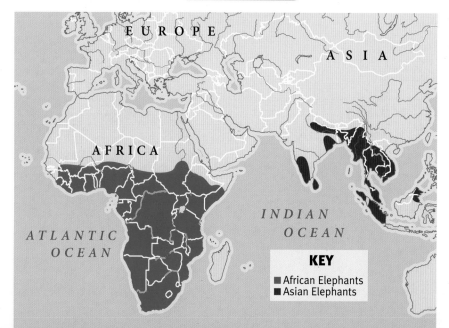

Elephant Range

EUROPE

ASIA

AFRICA

ATLANTIC OCEAN

INDIAN OCEAN

KEY
- African Elephants
- Asian Elephants

This map shows where elephants live in the wild.

Asian elephants are the second elephant species. Their **habitats** range from the Mekong River Basin in Southeast Asia to the eastern Himalayan Mountains. The three subspecies of Asian elephant are Indian, Sumatran, and Sri Lankan elephants. They're mainly found within Asia's forests.

Asian and African elephants share certain features. These include thick skin and a pair of tusks. All elephants also have a long, flexible trunk.

Tusks

Long trunk

Both species of elephants share certain features.

Thick skin

Some experts estimate that elephants may disappear in the next few decades.

Elephants at Risk

Poaching is one threat elephants face. Habitat loss is another. Such challenges have reduced elephant populations. As a result, Asian elephants are currently endangered. This means they are at very high risk of becoming **extinct**. The risk of extinction is slightly less for African elephants, which are considered vulnerable. That means the risk is not as severe but remains high.

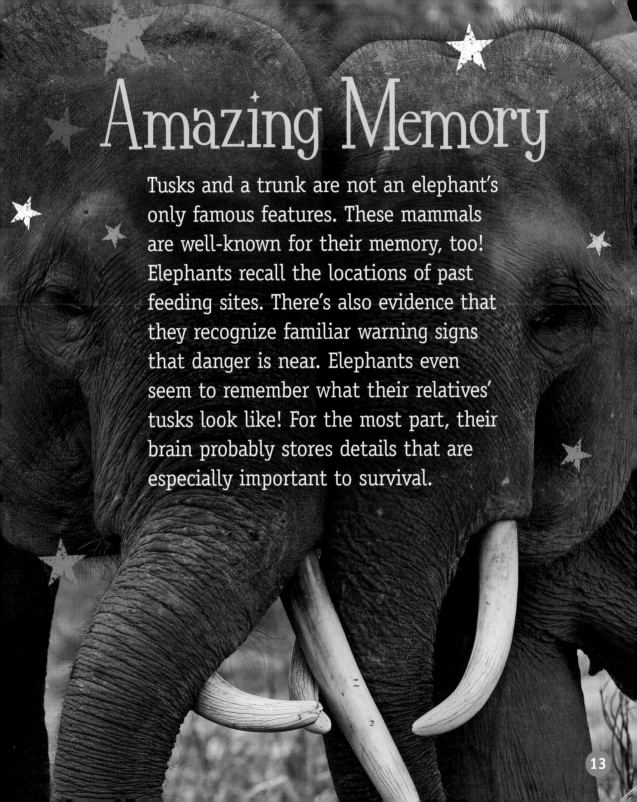

Amazing Memory

Tusks and a trunk are not an elephant's only famous features. These mammals are well-known for their memory, too! Elephants recall the locations of past feeding sites. There's also evidence that they recognize familiar warning signs that danger is near. Elephants even seem to remember what their relatives' tusks look like! For the most part, their brain probably stores details that are especially important to survival.

Two African elephant calves play.

Magnificent Mammals

Elephants are exceptional animals. Though these giants have many talents, sight is not one of them. They likely don't have good vision. Other senses, such as touch, make up for it. Elephants' skin may be 1.5 inches (3.8 centimeters) thick, but it is extremely sensitive! This helps elephants notice even small changes in their environment, such as a fly landing on the elephant's back. These animals are truly impressive from the ground up!

 Newborn elephants weigh 200 to 250 pounds (91 to 113 kilograms).

Gentle Giants

An elephant's exact size and appearance vary from subspecies to subspecies.

A COMPARISON OF ELEPHANT SUBSPECIES

Subspecies	Weight (Adults)	Habitat	Distinguishing Features
Forest elephant (African)	4,000 to 10,000 pounds (1,814 to 4,536 kg)	Rain forests	Compared to savanna elephant: straighter, thinner tusks; rounder ears; lighter coloring; less hair
Indian elephant (Asian)	5,000 to 9,000 pounds (2,268 to 4,082 kg)	Broadleaf forests and grasslands	Compared to other Asian subspecies: medium-sized ears; coloring darker than Sumatran but lighter than Sri Lankan elephants
Savanna elephant (African)	8,000 to 14,000 pounds (3,629 to 6,350 kg)	Grasslands	Compared to forest elephant: more curved, thicker tusks; more triangular ears; darker coloring; more hair
Sri Lankan elephant (Asian)	4,400 to 12,000 pounds (1,996 to 5,443 kg)	Broadleaf forests	Compared to other Asian subspecies: largest ears; darkest coloring
Sumatran elephant (Asian)	4,000 to 8,000 pounds (1,814 to 3,629 kg)	Broadleaf forests	Compared to other Asian subspecies: largest ears; darkest coloring

Elephants have toenails, just as humans do.

Tough Toes

An elephant basically walks on its tiptoes. Its foot bones are angled forward. The sole, or underside, of its feet is ridged, and the heel has a fatty pad of **tissue**. This foot structure helps an elephant avoid stumbling when it travels across bumpy or muddy ground. As it moves, the weight it puts on each foot is evenly distributed across its heel.

An elephant might flap its ears to keep cool.

Super Senses

With their large ears, elephants have impressive hearing. Their ears serve another purpose as well: They prevent overheating. Thousands of tiny blood vessels run just underneath the ear skin. As blood moves through these vessels, it cools. This helps control body temperature, keeping the elephant cool.

Elephants rely heavily on their nose, too. They can recognize certain smells as far away as 12 miles (19 kilometers)!

A Tremendous Trunk

An elephant's nostrils are at the end of its trunk, which forms part of its nose and upper lip. The trunk is made up of about 100,000 muscles and **tendons** that provide strength and flexibility. One to two fingerlike tips allow elephants to grasp and lift objects. When standing on their hind legs, they can use their trunk to reach leaves 19 feet (5.8 m) above the ground.

The fingerlike tips at the end of an elephant's trunk are very sensitive to touch.

Elephants also suck up water with their trunk. They then spray the water into their mouth or, if they want to cool down, across their body. An Asian elephant's trunk is capable of holding 2.2 gallons (8.3 liters) of water! Some elephants even swing their trunk at enemies like a weapon. Many also communicate by touching each other with the trunk or using it to create different sounds.

An elephant sprays water over a warthog and its young.

The shape of an African elephant's ears is similar to the shape of the African continent.

Tusks and Other Teeth

An elephant's tusks are two of its 26 teeth. Some tusks weigh as much as 220 pounds (100 kg) each! They're usually larger in males. African elephants have bigger tusks than Asian elephants.

Tusks are used by elephants as a weapon for self-defense. Elephants also use them to uproot plants. These mammals rely mainly on their other teeth to grind food. This food is typically fruit, twigs, bark, roots, and grasses.

Female elephants are very social and live within a herd all their lives.

A Look at Life Cycle

Wild elephants sometimes live 60 to 70 years. Most adult males, or bulls, prefer to live alone. Adult females, called cows, and younger elephants belong to **herds** of 8 to 100 animals. The oldest, largest cows generally lead such groups.

Cows have a baby, or calf, every four to five years. They carry the baby for 22 months before giving birth! That's the longest pregnancy of any mammal.

Growing Up in a Group

For more than two years, calves drink milk that their mother produces. Young elephants remain with their herd for far longer than that, though. Females frequently stay with the group for life. Some males don't leave until they're 15 years old.

Living in a herd offers elephants protection. Herd members help care for and protect one another. In the wild, healthy adults face few natural enemies. However, big cats, wild dogs, and even crocodiles attack calves and weaker elephants.

Adults protect calves in their herd from predators and other dangers.

Elephants sometimes turn everyday objects—such as this stick—into tools and toys.

Big and Brainy

Elephants are among Earth's most intelligent animals. They have a sharp memory and excellent problem-solving skills. They also make and use basic tools. Some even break apart sticks with their trunk to create simple fly swatters!

Elephants exhibit a wide range of emotions as well. At times, they're playful and affectionate. Yet they also mourn, or grieve, the death of other elephants.

Elephant Talk

Elephants express feelings like anger, fear, and excitement to each other in many different ways. Elephants rely on a variety of techniques to communicate. Communication often takes the form of movements and postures. Sometimes it is done with scents in natural substances produced by an elephant's body. Information is also exchanged through touch, vibration, and sound. The noises that elephants make include rumbles, cries, snorts, grunts, barks, and trumpeting calls.

Two elephants greet each other.

Big Animal, Big Impact

African elephants aren't just Earth's largest land animals. They're also a keystone species. That's a plant or animal that has a major impact on other species within its **ecosystem**. For savanna elephants, one big reason they're a keystone is that they keep grasslands from becoming forests.

WHAT'S A GRASSLAND WITHOUT GRASS?

Savanna elephants uproot trees and bushes as they eat. If this subspecies disappears, trees and bushes could become too tall or too thick. Their leaves and branches would block sunlight from reaching plants closer to the ground. Such plants include the grasses that fill the savanna ecosystem.

NOT GREAT FOR GRAZERS

The savanna serves as a habitat for several other species that graze, or eat grasses. Gazelles, zebras, and wildebeests are just a few animals that would be affected by any changes to savannas. If these grazers have less food, some might try to relocate. Not all of them would be successful or survive.

HARD ON HUNTERS

For big cats such as lions and cheetahs, if grazers disappear, so will their next meal. The same is true for jackals, hyenas, and crocodiles. With fewer grass-eating animals, these hunters would have to search elsewhere for food. Some of them already face the threat of extinction, so this could become a life-or-death challenge.

Most elephants eat hundreds of pounds of plant matter each day.

CHAPTER 3

An Uncertain Future

The extinction of either elephant species would be a tremendous loss for both humans and wildlife. People still have many unanswered questions about these intelligent, sensitive mammals. Elephants also influence wild ecosystems. Besides helping more light reach low-growing plants, they also spread seeds. As elephants roam, they drop food and produce waste. Such items contain seeds from the plants they eat. These seeds frequently develop into new plants.

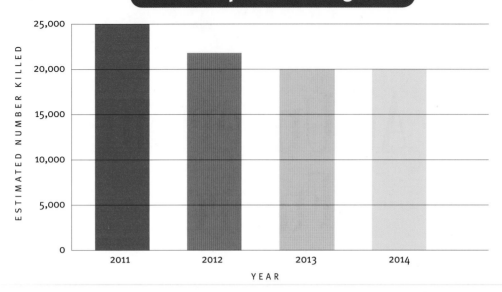

African Elephant Poaching Rates

ESTIMATED NUMBER KILLED

25,000

20,000

15,000

10,000

5,000

0

2011   2012   2013   2014

YEAR

The Illegal Ivory Trade

Between 2010 and 2012, roughly 100,000 African elephants were illegally killed for ivory. According to recent estimates, poachers in Africa kill as many as 100 of these majestic mammals each day.

International ivory trade has been banned since 1989. For a while, this seemed to be effective, and elephant populations were growing. However, both poaching and the demand for ivory rose, peaking in 2011 but staying high.

Why War Makes Things Worse

A further problem is that wars and political conflicts exist in some of the countries where poaching occurs. Governments are unable to spend as much time, effort, and money on enforcing antipoaching laws. It also leads to increased human traffic throughout the natural areas where elephants eat and **reproduce**.

Civil war has raged in and around what is now South Sudan for decades.

Too Little Living Space

Habitat loss threatens elephants, too. Throughout both Asia and Africa, people develop natural areas into farmland. They also allow livestock to overgraze, or feed too heavily on grasses and other plants. This limits food sources for elephants living today. Overgrazing has long-term effects as well. It causes the soil to wear away, which makes it more difficult for plants to grow in the future.

A rancher watches over his cattle in Ethiopia.

An Asian elephant walks through a rice field after farmers have harvested their crops.

Farmers vs. Elephants

With less space to live and less food to eat, elephants often wander onto farm fields. This fuels further tension between them and people. It is not unusual for a hungry herd of elephants to destroy an entire year's crop in just one night! In certain situations, elephants forced into close contact with humans will attack. Some farmers respond by poisoning or shooting them.

Vehicles stop to allow wild elephants to cross a road in India.

Habitats That Are Split Apart

The construction of roads, pipelines, railways, and buildings changes natural landscapes. This type of development fragments, or separates, elephant habitats. As a result, it becomes harder for these animals to locate new food and water sources. It is also more challenging for them to find **mates** outside of their immediate family. This results in too much **breeding** among relatives, which reduces a herd's overall health.

Wild Camera Work

Wildlife photographers produce images that provide people with important elephant updates. Sometimes their photos reveal information about the behavior and health of a specific herd. In other cases, they offer evidence of the harsh impacts of poaching and habitat loss. Wildlife photography is a rewarding career, but it isn't easy. Photographers need to know how to take pictures in a natural and often unpredictable setting.

Tracking collars provide valuable information about elephant habits.

A Chance to Change the Story

It's difficult to predict what the future will be for elephants. Only about 470,000 African elephants remain in the wild. Asian elephant populations are even lower. They currently stand at 40,000 to 50,000 animals.

Conservationists take many different actions to protect elephants. Some conservationists use tracking devices such as radio collars to monitor elephant populations. Others focus on creating and enforcing stricter antipoaching laws.

Learning to Live Together

Conservationists also try to preserve, or save, elephant habitats. They fight to increase the area of protected land and limit further land development. Just as importantly, they work with community members to find ways for people to live alongside elephants. For example, conservationists help form flying squads. These groups are made up of trained elephants and human riders. Flying squads drive wild elephants away from farms and villages and back into forests without injuring them.

An African Elephant Timeline

1500s
The African elephant population is estimated to be about 26 million.

1.5 million years ago
African elephants first appear.

Getting the Word Out

Effective conservation also relies on increased awareness. People of all ages and backgrounds need to understand the dangers that threaten elephants' survival. Programs and presentations at schools, nature centers, and zoos are a start. Rangers also educate the public about why elephants require and deserve protection. If such efforts are successful, these incredible animals will grace landscapes for centuries to come! ★

1913
Only about 10 million African elephants remain in the wild.

2002–2011
African forest elephant populations fall by 62 percent, from an estimated 260,000 to roughly 100,000.

2012
Ivory is sold for $1,000 per pound in China.

CALLING ALL CONSERVATIONISTS!

Conservationists represent all walks of life. Some are scientists. Others are kids just like you! What can you do to help? Here are a few ideas to get you started:

CELEBRATE AND REMEMBER

World Elephant Day is on August 12. You could visit elephants at the zoo with your family and friends. Or perhaps talk to a parent about writing to U.S. lawmakers. Remind these men and women that the international ivory trade is still a major concern. In fact, illegal ivory sales still occur within U.S. borders.

"ADOPT" AN ELEPHANT

For a small fee or donation, zoos and animal rescues sometimes allow people to "adopt" animals. Ask for help from a parent. You won't actually bring any elephants home. Instead, the money will help pay for their food, shelter, and care. You'll probably also receive photos and updates about your elephant.

TAKE "ELPHIES"

Talk to your teachers and student council about setting up a photo booth. Ask an adult to help students take "elphies." These are selfies that remind people of elephants. It can be as simple as posing with a stuffed elephant or holding up your own elephant drawing! Find out if you can print the photos and display them in your school. On poster board, write facts about elephant conservation to place with the elphies.

ASK AN EXPERT

With an adult's help, e-mail or write rangers who protect elephants. Ask what challenges their job involves and why they believe elephants are important. Or you can visit protected areas closer to home. Ask rangers there how they support local conservation efforts.

THE BIG DEBATE

Should All Ivory Be Illegal?

Buying and selling ivory internationally is currently illegal. However, not everyone agrees with the ban. Some people argue that allowing certain nations to sell ivory would help end the illegal market. Others insist that even partially legalizing the international ivory trade would further threaten conservation efforts.

Which side do you agree with? Why?

Yes Legalize part of the international ivory trade!

Because of the ban on international trade, the supply of ivory is limited. As a result, buyers are paying as much as $1,000 a pound or more for illegal products. Poachers continue hunting to make money. **New laws could allow people to sell tusks taken from elephants that died of natural causes.** Then the ivory trade wouldn't involve hunting. There would also be a greater supply of ivory. This would drive down prices and negatively affect poachers. Legalized ivory trade would give local residents a reason to fight poaching, too. Their future business would depend on healthy, stable elephant populations. A portion of the profit from the business could even fund conservation!

No Restrict the international ivory trade as much as possible!

Elephant populations are in crisis! It's too risky to experiment with an approach that might only create bigger problems. The illegal market for ivory will always exist. **Easing restrictions on international trade will simply provide poachers with new ways to make money.**

True, authorities could use high-tech tests to confirm a piece of ivory came from an elephant that died of natural causes. But will they want to spend the time and money to track every tusk? Plus, it's impossible to predict demand. How will authorities regulate sales if people want to purchase more ivory products? The risk to elephants is just too great!

Maximum thickness of elephant skin: 1.5 in. (3.8 cm)

Number of muscles and tendons that make up an elephant's trunk: About 100,000

Amount of water an Asian elephant's trunk can hold: 2.2 gal. (8.3 L)

Maximum weight of a single elephant tusk: 220 lb. (100 kg)

Life span of wild elephants: 60 to 70 years

Length of an elephant's pregnancy: 22 months

Number of African elephants that are poached daily: As many as 100

Number of African elephants that remain in the wild: About 470,000

Number of Asian elephants that remain in the wild: Between 40,000 and 50,000

Did you find the truth?

T Elephants may live up to 70 years in the wild.

F Poaching never occurs in protected areas.

Resources

Books

Claus, Matteson. *Animals and Deforestation*. New York: Gareth Stevens Publishing, 2014.

Furstinger, Nancy. *African Elephants*. Mankato, MN: The Child's World, 2015.

Hibbert, Clare. *Elephant Orphans*. New York: PowerKids Press, 2015.

McAneney, Caitlin, and Caitie McAneney. *How Elephants and Other Animals Hear the Earth*. New York: PowerKids Press, 2016.

Shea, Nicole. *Poaching and Illegal Trade*. New York: Gareth Stevens Publishing, 2014.

Visit this Scholastic Web site for more information about elephants and to download the Teaching Guide for this series:

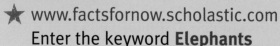 www.factsfornow.scholastic.com
Enter the keyword **Elephants**

Important Words

breeding (BREE-ding) mating and giving birth to young

conservation (kahn-sur-VAY-shuhn) the protection of valuable things, especially forests, wildlife, natural resources, or artistic or historic objects

ecosystem (EE-koh-sis-tuhm) all the living things in a place and their relation to the environment

extinct (ik-STINGKT) no longer found alive

habitats (HAB-uh-tats) the places where an animal or plant is usually found

herds (HURDZ) large groups of animals that stay together or move together

mates (MAYTS) animals that join together to reproduce

poachers (POH-churz) people who hunt or fish illegally

reproduce (ree-pruh-DOOS) to produce offspring

tendons (TEN-duhnz) strong, thick cords or bands of tissue that join a muscle to a bone or other body part

tissue (TISH-yoo) a mass of similar cells that form a particular part of an animal or plant

tusks (TUHSKS) the pair of long, curved, pointed teeth that stick out of the mouth of animals such as an elephant, walrus, or wild boar

Index

Page numbers in **bold** indicate illustrations.

About the Author

Katie Marsico graduated from Northwestern University and worked as an editor in reference publishing before she began writing in 2006. Since that time, she has published more than 200 titles for children and young adults. Ms. Marsico thinks elephants are among the most graceful, majestic animals she has ever seen.